MEN-AT-ARMS SERIES

EDITOR: MARTIN WINDROW

Queen Victoria's Enemies (1): Southern Africa

Text by IAN KNIGHT

Colour plates by RICHARD SCOLLINS

CW00953873

OSPREY PUBLISHING LONDON

Published in 1989 by
Osprey Publishing Ltd
59 Grosvenor Street, London W1X 9DA
© Copyright 1989 Osprey Publishing Ltd

British Library Cataloguing in Publication Data

Knight, Ian
Victoria's enemies.—(Men-at-arms, 212)
1: Southern Africa
1. Military forces, Southern Africa, 1800–1900
I. Title   II. Series
355′.00968

ISBN 0-85045-901-X

Filmset in Great Britain
Printed through Bookbuilders Ltd, Hong Kong

Artist's Note

Readers may care to note that the original paintings
from which the colour plates in this book were
prepared are available for private sale. All
reproduction copyright whatsoever is retained by the
publisher. All enquiries should be addressed to:

Richard Scollins
14 Ladywood Road,
Ilkeston,
Derbyshire.

The publishers regret that they can enter into no
correspondence upon this matter.

Acknowledgements

Thanks to Brian Maggs for allowing me access to his
splendid photographic collection, and to Claire
Colbert and George Rice for their help with the
photographic copying.

Author's Note

This series is intended to complement Michael
Barthorp's *The British Army on Campaign 1816–1902*.
Details of British uniforms in the Cape Frontier and
Basotho Wars can be found in MAA 193, *(1):
1816–1853*. The 1881 Transvaal War is covered in
MAA 196, *(3): 1856–1881*, and the Ndebele Rebellion
and Anglo-Boer War in MAA 201, *(4): 1882–1902*.

Queen Victoria's Enemies (1): Southern Africa

Introduction

When Queen Victoria acceded to the British throne in June 1837, British troops had recently concluded a war in southern Africa against the Xhosa people, and the seeds were already sown for a clash with the Boers. When she died in January 1901 Britain was once more fighting the Boers, in one of the longest and costliest of the Imperial Colonial Wars. Southern Africa had proved a cockpit of tension and conflict second only to the Indian sub-continent. The causes of these troubles lay in the opposing interests of a variety of competing colonies, independent white republics, and black African states. This book will attempt to outline the history of this strife, and to describe the military systems of Queen Victoria's many enemies in southern Africa.

Europeans first established themselves on the very tip of the African continent in 1652, when the Dutch set up a way-station at the Cape of Good Hope to service their fleets on the long haul to India. The Dutch found the indigenous in-habitants, the semi-nomadic Khoi ('Hottentots') and San ('Bushmen'), easy to evict; but they were not interested in the costly process of exploring the hinterland. Strict prohibitions were placed on the Dutch settlers allowed to cultivate produce on the fringes of the Colony, but their hardy lifestyle

A sketch of bush fighting in the Sixth Cape Frontier war, which suggests something of the nature of such warfare. Note that the Xhosa are armed with flintlock muskets. (Author's collection)

encouraged in these people an independent spirit. By the 18th century these frontier farmers, called 'Boers' then, and more frequently today 'Afrikaners', were wandering steadily eastward in search of new pastures. Along the banks of the Great Fish River, they received something of a shock: they met black Africans coming in the other direction.

The Africans had crossed the Limpopo River into South Africa centuries before. They had populated the landscape, wandering as their herds needed fresh grass, in two related cultural groups. The Sotho had occupied the high-veld plateau of the interior, and the Nguni had drifted down the rolling grasslands of the eastern coast, cut off from the interior by the Drakensberg Mountains. It was an Nguni group, the Xhosa, who encountered the frontier Boers. Early relations were peaceful, but the two cultures were basically in competition for the same natural resource—land. As early as 1779,

there were skirmishes, though these amounted to little more than cattle-raids.

The British came to the Cape in 1805, inheriting it as one of the political prizes of the Napoleonic Wars. Over the next century, their policy would vacillate with successive home governments, but the overwhelming imperative was to protect the strategic route to India, whilst incurring as little expense as possible within the colony. Inevitably, however, the hopelessly confused border situation dragged in British troops as Imperial policemen; and the Boers soon developed a marked distaste for British authority.

The situation was further complicated on the eve of Queen Victoria's reign by two violent migrations. The first was the series of wars which marked the rise of the Zulu empire in the 1820s (known as the *mfecane* in Nguni, and *difaqane* in Sotho), and which replaced the original African clan system with a

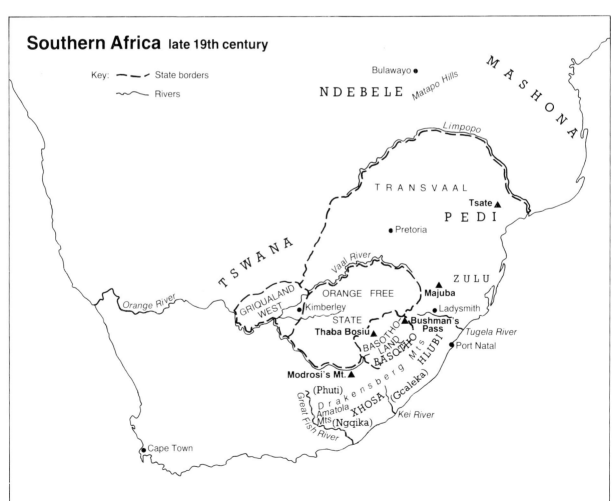

Southern Africa late 19th century

Key: — · — State borders
~~~ Rivers

4

number of militarily strong kingdoms. The second was the Great Trek of the 1830s, when Boer families packed their possessions into ox-wagons and 'trekked' away from British rule, establishing independent territories beyond the Orange and Vaal rivers. Britain regarded the Trekkers as British subjects, and Boer clashes with the new African kingdoms inevitably provoked a British reaction.

From the 1820s, too, there was increased British economic involvement in southern Africa, initially in the persons of immigrant farmers, imported in a somewhat cynical attempt to pacify the Cape Frontier, and later in the mining industry which followed the discovery of diamonds near Kimberley in 1867. The resulting pressure for land and African labour led to a heightening of tension with the African states, stimulated by the miners' practice of paying for black labour with firearms. The result was a series of conflicts in the 1870s, when British and Colonial authorities sought to break the power of African states and disarm their warriors.

An attempt to deal with this chaotic and dangerous situation by a policy of confederation, uniting the disparate groups under British rule, collapsed following the costly war against the Zulus in 1879, and the rejection of the policy by the Boer republic of the Transvaal, which manifested itself in the 1881 Transvaal War.

Following the problems of the 1870s, Britain attempted to keep southern Africa at arm's length; but the discovery of gold in the Transvaal in 1885 intensified economic and political competition, and ushered in a decade in which Britain attempted to isolate the Boer republic and thereby acquire some influence over her natural resources. An important figure in this manoeuvring was the diamond magnate Cecil Rhodes. In 1890 Rhodes' British South Africa Company occupied Mashonaland, part of modern Zimbabwe, a move which was to lead to war with both the local African groups, the Ndebele and Mashona. In 1895 Rhodes' lieutenant, Dr Jameson, led his famous raid into the Transvaal in an attempt to precipitate a miners' *coup*. It failed miserably, and relations between the British and Boers deteriorated to such an extent that the Boer War broke out in 1899. There were to be three bitter years of fighting before the Boer republics were defeated.

Xhosa warriors ambushing a British column, Eighth War. This picture captures very well the terrain to which the Xhosa adapted their tactics. Note use of 'musket rest'. (Author's collection)

A posed study of a Xhosa warrior in traditional dress. His shield is of the Natal or 'Zulu' type, introduced amongst the Xhosa by Mfengu refugees. (Author's collection)

Chronology

The following is a list of the main campaigns fought by British and Colonial troops in southern Africa between 1837 and 1902. A number of small expeditions (e.g. the Black Flag Rebellion, 1875) have not been included, nor have campaigns waged by the Boer (Afrikaner) Republics against Africans, although some of these are referred to in the text.

1842: Port Natal Expedition.
1845: Zwartkopjes Expedition.
1846–7: 7th Cape Frontier War[1] ('The War of the Axe').
1848: Boomplaats Expedition.
1850–53: 8th Cape Frontier War.
1852: Berea Expedition, Basotholand.
1873: Langalibalele Rebellion.
1877–8: 9th Cape Frontier War.
1878: First Tswana Expedition (Griqualand West); first (British) Sekhukhune Expedition.
1879: Moorosi's Rebellion.
1879: Anglo-Zulu War.
1879: Second (British) Sekhukhune Expedition.
1880–1: Basotho Gun War.

1881: Transvaal War.
1888: Dinuzulu Rebellion, Zululand.
1893: Ndebele War.
1895: Jameson's Raid.
1896–7: Ndebele and Mashona Rebellion.
1896–7: Second Tswana Expedition (Bechuanaland).
1899–1902: Anglo-Boer War.

The Xhosa

The Xhosa were in the vanguard of the Nguni southward drift, and so were the first to feel the pinch as two alien cultures competed for the same land. Although the initial contact took place along the banks of the Great Fish River, adventurous bands of both Boers and Xhosa soon crossed over, and the settlement pattern overlapped. Significantly, the first Cape Frontier War (1779–81)—little more than a skirmish—resulted from a dispute over pasturage. The response of the Colonial authorities was to designate a fixed border, and this was to become the cornerstone of subsequent British policy. But neither the Xhosa—used to moving their herds as different grasses matured throughout the year—nor the free-spirited Boers, could be completely restrained.

There were to be eight further Cape Frontier Wars (1793, 1799–1802, 1811–12, 1818–19, 1834–35, 1846–47, 1850–53, and 1877–8) of increasing severity; although each war had its individual causes, and both sides complained of provocation and injustice, the consistent Colonial intention was to contain the Xhosa. The wars reversed the Nguni advance, and by the end of the 19th century the Xhosa had seen much of their best land settled by whites. The Eighth War was long, bitter and decisive, the Xhosa being defeated at last by a campaign of attrition waged against their civilian population and crops.[2]

The national grief manifested itself in a suicidal religious delusion: Xhosa seers urged believers to slaughter their herds in sacrifice to bring back long dead heroes who would sweep the white man into the sea. The Xhosa killed their cattle, but the chiefs

[1]The Cape Frontier Wars were formerly known as the 'Kaffir Wars', after the old European term for the Xhosa. Since the term 'kaffir' has now acquired derogatory connotations, however, it has not been used here.

[2]See *Military Illustrated* magazine, No. 14, for a brief account of the career of the Xhosa war-leader Maqoma.

did not rise, and the people starved. The final Cape Frontier War in 1877–8 was little more than a last proud gesture of defiance, ruthlessly suppressed.

The Xhosa did not boast a strong centralised state like their northern cousins the Zulus. The nation consisted of a number of clan groups, family units who traced their origins to a common ancestor. The amaTshawe clan had become dominant in the 17th century, and the chiefs of the amaTshawe were regarded as paramount chiefs of the nation as a whole. However, although the paramount chief had a number of important political and cultural functions, his power was far from absolute. Most clan chiefs ruled with a degree of independence accorded by the strength of their following—the most powerful could, and did, ignore the dictates of the paramount. In fact, the Xhosa state had a tendency to expansion through fragmentation, each son of a chief being encouraged to set up a chieftainship of his own. This process in itself sent Xhosa bands across the frontier; but it was aggravated early in the 19th century by a severe

succession dispute which split the nation into two sections.

The paramount traditionally lived east of the Kei River, but a large group, contesting his authority, crossed into the land between the Kei and the Fish. The paramount's section became known as the *amaGcaleka* ('the people of Gcaleka', the name of the paramount), while the other section became known as the *amaNgqika* ('Ngqika's people', after their principal leader). Fighting caused by this rift also overflowed into the Colony. Although the Ngqika acknowledged the technical authority of the paramount, they acted largely independently, and were to bear the brunt of the conflict with the Europeans. Not that the Colonial authorities always recognised the distinction: in 1835 the paramount Hintsa was shot apparently under treacherous circumstances by the British, who were

A war dance of Gcaleka Xhosa, *c.*1877. The warriors are wearing traditional hide cloaks, with the hair on the inside, and turned out at the top. Note the headcloth on the man in the foreground. (Author's collection)

convinced he was the real instigator of the Fifth War. Generally the paramounts avoided too open support for the Ngqika, although individual Gcaleka chiefs did take part in the fighting. In 1877, however, Hinsta's son, Sahrili, openly committed himself to the Ninth War, and British troops were faced with combined Xhosa armies larger than any previously fielded. It was too late, however, to reverse the course of events, since by then the Xhosa were hopelessly outclassed by their enemy's firepower.

Such divisions did not make for a standing army. Each grown man was a warrior. When a chief decided on war, he would give the command '*ilizwe ilfile*'—'the land is dead'—and the warriors would be summoned by a distinctive keening cry passed by women from hill-top to hill-top.

Costume and Weapons

The warriors would muster in their everyday dress. This might consist of as little as a penis-sheath, although it was usual to wear a cloak of bullock-hide. This was worked to great suppleness, and worn with the hair on the inside, the outside being coloured with red ochre. Ochre was also a favourite human cosmetic, worked into the skin with animal fat to produce a deep copper glow. Men ornamented themselves with beads around the head, neck and waist, and great hunters might wear ivory armlets or leopard's-teeth necklaces from animals they had killed, to assume the fierce qualities of their prey. Magic and ritual were an important part of warfare, with diviners specialising in the art attempting to enhance the warriors' strength and courage and to undermine that of the enemy. Most warriors went into battle bare-headed; but some young men in the early wars wore an extravagant headdress of wing feathers upright above the temples, while single crane feathers were given to men who had particularly distinguished themselves. Chiefs wore cloaks of leopardskin, and brass armbands on the right arm.

Traditional weapons consisted of spears, a simple club with a burled, polished head, and a shield. The principal spear was the *intshuntshe*, a light throwing spear with a long shaft and a leaf-shaped blade. It could be thrown with some accuracy and force up to 30 or 40 metres, and was thrown with a quivering motion which added to its penetrating power on impact. One variation of the throwing spear was simply a sharpened metal tang mounted on a shaft; and spears with serrated edges were not unknown. A warrior would charge down on his enemy, holding a bundle of seven or eight spears in his left hand, and throwing with his right. The last spear would be retained in case the order '*Phakathi!*'—'Get inside!'—was given, to signal a rush to hand-to-hand combat. Sometimes the shaft of the last spear might be broken off to make it easier for stabbing, or sometimes a spear with a larger blade would be used. Generally, however, Xhosa tactics did not encourage close-quarter combat, as each warrior was expected to skirmish according to his individual talents.

Traditional Xhosa shields were large cowhide ovals, big enough to cover three-quarters of the body. The hair was left on the outside, but the colour had no significance. A pole ran up the back of the shield, and was held in place by leather thongs

A Xhosa headdress of grey wing feathers, worn by some young warriors. (Exeter Museum)

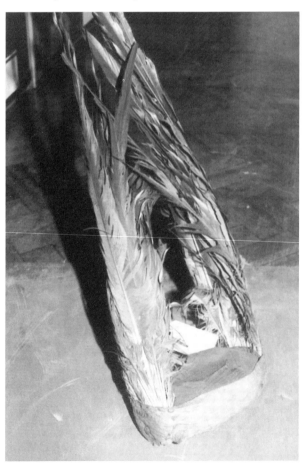

A Xhosa war dance in the Amatola Mountains, Eighth Frontier War, painted by Thomas Baines, who was a witness to much of the fighting. Note both traditional Xhosa headdresses and European clothes. (Africana Museum, Johannesburg)

bound through holes pierced in the hide. From the 1820s large numbers of refugees from the Zulu wars in Natal, known as *mfengu*, settled amongst the Xhosa, and they brought with them the familiar Zulu-pattern shield, with its tight lacing and fur crest on top of the pole. Although both types were apparently carried as late as 1877, shields became less popular once it was realised that they did not deflect bullets, and were an encumbrance in the bush. Instead the cloak was wrapped round the left arm and held across the body to protect it.

Tactics

Early Xhosa battles were fought in the open, with a standard battlefield tactic rather similar to the Zulu 'beast's horns' encircling movement. Young warriors formed a central body, with senior men forming *amaphiko*, 'wings', on either side. The chief fought with a body known as the *amafanenkhosi*, 'those who die with the chief', but, while he was expected to show daring and courage, he was not expected to expose himself needlessly. Indeed, the Xhosa were appalled when Europeans attacked or killed chiefs without compunction. These traditional tactics were soon abandoned, however, once the Xhosa realised their ineffectiveness in the face of heavy firepower, and they turned instead to guerrilla tactics. Indeed, they proved extremely adept at meeting new challenges, and chose as their battleground natural strongholds, like the Amatola Mountains, a maze of intersecting ridges and bush-choked valleys.

From these refuges they would launch offensive sweeps into Colonial territory, retreating before they could be pinned down. They became expert at separating small enemy parties, cutting them off, surrounding them and destroying them. Individual warriors or herds of cattle were used as decoys—on one occasion a party of soldiers fired at a lone warrior, and before they could reload the Xhosa burst from the bush and overwhelmed them. It was quite common for the Xhosa to taunt their enemy, not merely to add an element of personal challenge, but to tempt them to break formation. Unencumbered in the bush, living off the land, the Xhosa could move easily through a landscape the Europeans considered impenetrable.

The cumbersome British supply wagons soon became a target for the Xhosa, who laid efficient ambushes, striking the trains as they wound along steep tracks bordered on both sides by bush. The Xhosa would kill the oxen to immobilise the

Sandile, chief of the Ngqika Xhosa from 1840 to 1878, who was killed in action in the Ninth War. His dress is the leopardskin cloak of a chief. (Africana Museum, Johannesburg)

powder was coarse and strong. Bullets were improvised from whatever material came to hand—when one mission station was overrun in a raid, lead from the printing press was melted down to make bullets, and pages from Bibles were pressed into service as wadding. With no one to train them, Xhosa warriors fired from the hip, or held the butt away from the shoulder to avoid the recoil: small wonder that Xhosa fire was held to be ineffective beyond 50 yards, and several British commentators who had been on the receiving end expressed the view that the spear was both more effective and more terrifying.

The Xhosa somehow lacked the glamour of their Zulu cousins, whose discipline and massed charges excited the admiration of their enemies, and thereby ensured lasting fame. Yet the Xhosa had a distinct military genius of their own, a flexibility, ingenuity and tenacity which was ideally suited to their environment, and which proved consistently hard to suppress.

The Basotho

The *mfecane* effectively smashed the Sotho clan system in southern Africa's interior. In 1822 several powerful groups of refugees were driven over the Drakensberg Mountains by the Zulu wars on the coastal strip. At least partially armed and organised on the Zulu pattern, they fell on the weaker Sotho clans, raiding their cattle and crops and driving them out. This set off a fearsome chain reaction, in which dispossessed clans attacked one another, until the interior was occupied largely by bands of restless marauders.

From this debris, a young chief named Moshoeshoe built the Basotho nation. Moshoeshoe's clan had been driven from its lands like the others, and wandered in the western foothills of the Drakensberg until Moshoeshoe discovered a large flat-topped hill called *Thaba Bosiu*, 'The Mountain at Night'. Such hills are a feature of the district, and Thaba Bosiu is a natural fortress. About four miles in circumference, it rises 400 feet from the plain, and is surrounded by cliffs, broken by only six easily-defensible passes to the summit. From this stronghold Moshoeshoe was able to repel both

wagons, and attack the least-protected part of the line, hoping to cut off the escort as they struggled to move up. Inevitably, while the Xhosa were usually able to count on the element of surprise, European movements were always clear to them; they used a simple system of hill-top signal fires to alert one another to enemy progress. It is no coincidence that from the War of the Axe (the 7th War), the British struck increasingly at Xhosa homesteads and crops: it was easier to starve the warriors out of their strongholds than to flush them out.

From the 1830s the Xhosa began to acquire both horses and guns. They never developed a cavalry arm, considering it impractical in bush warfare, but individuals such as chiefs and spies were quick to appreciate the potential for extra mobility. Guns were first taken from whites killed in battle, but illegal gun-running steadily increased as thousands of obsolete Brown Bess muskets were dumped on unsophisticated native markets across the world in the aftermath of the Napoleonic Wars. In the 7th, 8th and 9th Wars, guns were a crucial part of Xhosa tactical thinking. Most guns, however, were of the poorest quality, spare parts were unobtainable, and

Sotho and Nguni attackers, and it became a rallying place for Sotho refugees from all over the interior.

Moshoeshoe's nation-building techniques were in marked contrast to those of his Nguni rivals such as Shaka. Although he was not averse to cattle-raiding to increase his power and prestige, Moshoeshoe was a diplomatic and compassionate man, who welcomed new adherents, and avoided many a conflict by calculated humility. As his kingdom grew, Moshoeshoe's people abandoned the names of their original clans and took to calling themselves *Basotho*, simply 'The Sotho'.

Moshoeshoe's kingdom lay 100 miles beyond the Orange River, the northern boundary of the Cape Colony; but even before the Great Trek adventurous Boers had been drifting towards Basotholand. During the 1830s the bulk of the Trekkers passed him by, en route for the lands across the Vaal, but enough stayed to sow the seeds of future conflicts. The issue, as ever, was land. Moshoeshoe was content to let Europeans occupy parts of his territory, as long as they were content to live peacefully alongside the Sotho. Gradually, however, as the Boers came to assume permanent rights to their settlements, and the land began to fill up with both Sotho, attracted to Moshoeshoe, and the ever expanding Boers, tension mounted.

Moshoeshoe appealed to the British to intervene, since many of the whites were British subjects; and the eccentric Governor of the Cape, Sir Harry Smith, rashly annexed the land north of the Orange as the Orange River Sovereignty in 1848. This was to have unforeseen consequences for the Sotho, when the subsequent British inquiry into disputed land adopted a distinctly hostile posture, and proposed boundaries which Moshoeshoe found impossible to accept. An attempt was made to force the issue, and a small unit of British regulars, supported by Boers and African allies, advanced into Basotholand.

In June 1851, at a hill called Viervoet, the Basotho used a cattle decoy to lure away their African enemies, then trapped them above a line of cliffs and severely mauled them. A spirited attack then drove the regulars and Boers from the field. Only Moshoeshoe's subsequent restraint prevented his followers from raiding across the Sovereignty. British policy in the region was called into question by the defeat. In March 1852 Sir Harry Smith was recalled, discredited by Viervoet and by a far more serious war against the Xhosa. His successor, Sir George Cathcart, thought it necessary that the Basotho be shown the might of the British Empire; and in December 1852, having failed to intimidate Moshoeshoe diplomatically, he advanced on Thaba Bosiu.

At the Berea Heights his troops ascended a hill to round up a herd of cattle, and were promptly surrounded by the Sotho and trapped against the cliffs. Several small parties of Lancers were wiped out. When the Basotho pressed home their attack

Chief Moshoeshoe, the founder of the Basotho nation, photographed in the 1860s at a time when his people were involved in a prolonged struggle with both British and Boers. (Africana Museum, Johannesburg)

Thaba Bosiu, Moshoeshoe's stronghold, typical of the mountain retreats of the southern Sotho. This illustration shows one of the passes leading to the summit. (Author's collection)

only a determined stand prevented them from overrunning the rest of the force. Cathcart was faced with a humiliating retreat, but Moshoeshoe's diplomacy allowed him to save face. The king, though clearly master of the field, sent a message offering his submission and promising to support British policy in the future. It allowed Cathcart a way out, and the second expedition against the Basotho withdrew.

Once more, however, the consequences were unfortunate for the Basotho. Exasperated by the cost and complexity of its involvement beyond the Orange, Britain promptly abandoned the Sovereignty, handing it over with embarrassing haste to the Boers, who renamed it the Orange Free State. Since Britain did not resolve the border question before she left, Moshoeshoe merely found himself facing the Boers over the same problem. In 1858 the Free State tried to force the Basotho to accept restricted boundaries; but the subsequent expedition failed to capture Thaba Bosiu, and when the Sotho raided farms behind Boer lines, the offensive collapsed as the farmers returned to protect their homes. In 1865 the Free State tried again, and there was a much more determined attempt to take the Basotho strongholds. It failed, but Boer attacks on

Sotho crops threatened to starve Moshoeshoe into submission. Reluctantly the king agreed to Boer demands, but then appealed once more to Britain. This time he was successful: in 1868 Britain annexed Basotholand. Moshoeshoe, one of the most remarkable African leaders to emerge from the *mfecane*, died shortly afterwards.

Yet there was to be one last struggle between the Basotho and the British Empire. In 1871 Basotholand was given over to the Cape Colony, which had recently been granted responsible government. In 1879 the Colony passed the Disarmament Act, under which all Africans within its boundaries were required to give up their firearms. This included the Basotho. Since many were disillusioned with white promises of protection, remembering how only their guns had saved them when they had been abandoned to their enemies before, a sizeable party, led by Moshoeshoe's son Masopha and grandson Lerothodi, refused to comply. The result was the Gun War, which broke out in 1880. Fighting was extensive and confused, with the Basotho laying siege to magistracies and other centres of Colonial authority. The Colony put large numbers of troops in the field but the Sotho remained on the offensive, launching lightning attacks on the British columns, yet seldom committing themselves to a pitched battle in the open. As fighting dragged on into 1881, negotiations opened which finally brought the war to a halt: the Sotho were not broken, nor were they required to surrender their guns. On balance, their record in the field against Europeans, whether British or Boer, was remarkably good.

Organisation

In traditional Sotho society clan armies were organised along age-regiment lines. When about 18 or 19, Sotho youths would be grouped together for the ceremonies of initiation into manhood, and this bound them with ties of loyalty which lasted throughout life. Initiates of the same age-group would fight together as a military unit. This is, of course, similar to the familiar Zulu system, although amongst the Sotho the degree of militarisation was less pronounced. Sotho regiments had names—Moshoeshoe's own was the *Matlama*, 'The Binders'—but they were not quartered in barracks like the Zulu *amabutho*, nor do they seem to have worn distinctive unit costumes. This system seems to have been adapted to take account of the large numbers of refugees from broken clans who initially made up the Basotho. When, however, intact clans offered their allegiance to Moshoeshoe they were accepted into the kingdom as vassals, and allowed to retain their own regiments, who were nonetheless expected to muster at the king's bidding.

Although Moshoeshoe's sons were strategically placed around the kingdom as centres of royal authority, the Sotho kingdom was much less centralised than the Zulu. Moshoeshoe often had difficulty controlling his subordinates, and outsiders were sometimes able to exploit internal divisions. Towards the end of his reign, Moshoeshoe's sons, eager to establish their own prestige, proved particularly troublesome.

Warriors were trained in the art of war at the initiation schools, and young men were expected to establish themselves by some daring exploit. Before the *mfecane*, therefore, warfare amounted to little more than cattle-raiding, as newly formed regiments sought to enrich themselves at a rival's expense. Casualties were few, and villages and crops were seldom touched. The brutal style of total war

A Basotho warrior, as he would have looked in the mid-19th century. He is wearing traditional Sotho dress—note the winged shield and assegai quiver—but has already acquired a horse and gun. (McGregor Museum)

imported by the Nguni ushered in an age of fighting for survival, but the earlier chivalry did not totally vanish from Moshoeshoe's outlook.

Costume and Weapons

Clothing for Sotho men was a knotted breech-cloth of animal hide and perhaps a skin cloak fastened on the right shoulder. In war, men wore a large ball of black ostrich feathers on top of the head, fastened by a string under the chin. Warriors of rank or renown were permitted to wear cloaks of leopard-skin. These seem to have had holes cut in the sides, through which the arms were thrust. Senior men also wore a curious gorget, a 'V' shaped piece of thin flat brass, suspended from a thong around the neck

Old and new traditions: Chief Masopha (right), Moshoeshoe's son and an important Basotho leader in the Gun War, in European dress, and his standard bearer in the traditional costume of a warrior of rank. Note the metal breast-plate or gorget, and the feathered shield stick which served as the 'standard'. (Author's collection)

so as to hang over the throat and upper chest.

Weapons consisted of a bundle of light throwing spears, with small blades and long shafts, carried in a leather quiver over the shoulder, and a wooden club. Shields were of cow-hide, and curiously shaped with two projecting wings on either side. They were stiffened by a stick at the back, which was topped with a crest of fur or black ostrich feathers. A chief might have a particularly long shield-stick projecting two or even three feet above the shield, with an ostentatious plume. This served as a rallying point or standard in a mêlée. Generally hand-to-hand fighting was avoided, as the spears were unsuitable for stabbing, and the shield, designed to deflect spears in flight, was inadequate protection at close quarters.

Although traditional Sotho dress and armament continued well into the second half of the 19th century, the variety of opposition faced by the Basotho led to fundamental changes. In the 1830s Moshoeshoe had clashed with both the Tlokwa, a rival Sotho group who had acquired a particularly grim reputation in the *mfecane*; and the Griqua, descendants of the Khoi, the original displaced inhabitants of the Cape. The Tlokwa included battle-axes in their armament—half-moon metal blades on the end of a tang, sunk into a wooden handle—and these were adopted by the Basotho. The Griqua used horses and guns which they had acquired from the Boers; these, too, Moshoeshoe adopted.

The Basotho were unique amongst southern African blacks in that they possessed horses in large numbers, and became so good at handling them that one British officer likened them to the cossacks. The horses were originally a mixed breed, but soon developed a characteristic strain known as the 'Basotho pony'. Small and sure-footed, they were ideally suited to their hilly environment. Initially the warriors rode bare-back, but with increased contact with Europeans, saddles and bridles became more available.

And so it was with guns. The Basotho first obtained them from fallen Griqua, but they were astute enough to realise their potential and by the mid-century had acquired large numbers from gun runners. The problems were the same as for the Xhosa, however: the guns were obsolete and of poor quality, and powder, ammunition and training was scarce. In the early clashes with the British and the Free State Boers, Basotho riflemen were hopelessly outclassed. Their aim was wild, and their bullets fell short. In one of the early engagements of the war of 1865 some 2,000 Sotho charged to within 100 yards of a Boer line and loosed a volley—which hit only one horse. When the Boers returned the fire, they killed 65 Sotho. By comparison, when the Sotho managed to cut off a party of Boers in 1858, they were able to kill 15 and wound five more, using mainly spears and axes. Nevertheless, the Basotho made serious efforts to improve their firepower—in 1865 they even had six cannon acquired from smugglers, as well as a 3pdr. cast in Basotholand under European supervision. The problems of powder and training remained, however; the cannon were seldom used and easily put out of action.

By the time of the Gun War the situation had begun to change. Diggers at Kimberley were offering a gun in payment for a season's work, and modern breech-loaders such as Sniders and Enfields attracted more labourers than antiquated flint-locks. Other new labour-intensive industries, such as building railways, did not pay in guns, but it was relatively easy for workers to exchange their wages for them at stores along the route home. Despite official disapproval of this trade, and a fear of black uprising amongst the settlers, it was particularly effective at securing labour. So many guns passed into African hands that the Sotho came to regard possession of a gun as an essential mark of manhood.

The acquisition of large numbers of guns and horses affected Basotho tactics in the later wars. Moshoeshoe had used a combination of the offensive raid and defensive withdrawal to natural strongholds. On foot, Basotho infantry moved swiftly, keeping as much as possible to natural cover. At both Viervoet and Berea they successfully used cattle as a decoy, then lay in wait to ambush the enemy when he broke formation. In both cases natural obstacles, reinforced with stone walls, were used to trap the enemy, who were overwhelmed in a rush. In the first war against the Free State, Sotho bands slipped round behind the Boer lines, and the threat to their homes was sufficient to cause the Boers to call off the attack. When pressed themselves, the Basotho would retire to their mountain strongholds, of which Thaba Bosiu

Chief Lerothodi, Moshoeshoe's grandson, another important leader in the Gun War. He is wearing the straw hat and blanket typical of the later period. (Author's collection)

"Blanket boys" is a name for the Basotho

remained an impenetrable bastion. The passes were blocked, and defenders poured stones, shot and spears down on the attackers. Despite many attempts, neither black nor white antagonists succeeded in storming Thaba Bosiu.

By the 1850s the horse and gun were already making their mark, and they dominated the Gun War. The standard Sotho tactic was to mass out of sight of the enemy, then charge down furiously, loosing a volley at close range. This had little effect on regular troops in formation; but when perfected during the Gun War, such ambushes could devastate the unprepared. Lerothodi began the Gun War with a massed frontal attack on the magistracy at Mafeteng, but was repulsed with heavy loss. The Sotho learned from the mistake, and in a successful ambush at Qalabane in October 1880 killed 32 Cape Yeomanry in a lightning charge. While the Colonial forces were badly handled, Masopha and Lerothodi led the Basotho with skill and daring. They were still in the field under arms when a peace settlement was agreed.

The appearance of the Sotho had changed by this time, too. Some were wearing pieces of European clothing, and many wore a high-crowned, wide-brimmed straw hat, said to have been inspired by early contact with Boer headgear. Woollen blankets, with characteristic striped patterns and fastened by a pin on the right shoulder, were universal. As well as their guns, they carried the traditional leather quiver with a variety of spears, axes and clubs. Ostrich plumes and shields were still in use in the 1850s and '60s, but are seldom mentioned in accounts of the Gun War.

Moorosi's Rebellion

Shortly before the outbreak of the Gun War, Colonial forces found themselves committed to a small but tough campaign to suppress Chief Moorosi of the Phuthi clan. Although usually referred to as Basotho, the Phuthi were originally an Nguni clan who had crossed the Drakensberg long before the *mfecane*. Though they retained elements of Nguni culture, they had become increasingly influenced by the Sotho. Moorosi's lands lay south of the Orange River, on the fringes of Moshoeshoe's territory; but Moorosi was regarded as a Basotho vassal, and the Phuthi were particularly active allies during the early wars of Moshoeshoe's reign.

In 1877 the Colonial Government allocated Moorosi's district a new magistrate, whose heavy-handed methods of tax-collection upset the Phuthi. Moorosi's own son, Doda, was arrested early in 1878; escaping from jail on 1 January 1879, he took refuge at his father's stronghold. This was a flat-topped mountain, about one mile long and half a mile wide, overlooking the Orange River. Like all such Sotho strongholds, it was ringed with cliffs at the summit, with only a few guarded points of access. The Colonial authorities demanded that Moorosi surrender his son. This order, coming at the same time as Colonial demands that all Sotho should give up their arms, seemed to be part of a

Basotho under fire in the Gun War. Many are wearing items of **European clothing, but traditional breech-hides are still in evidence. (Author's collection)**

The death of Chief Moorosi of the Phuthi during the storming of 'Moorosi's Mountain'. Both Africans are wearing European clothes and carrying firearms. (Author's collection)

wider plan to undermine the authority of the chiefs. Moorosi refused; the Colonial authorities decided to make an example of him, and on 24 March troops advanced against Moorosi's Mountain.

The Phuthi had only 200 or 300 fighting men on the mountain, but they were particularly well armed, and Moorosi had been stockpiling ammunition as tension mounted. (It seems unlikely that the Phuthi would have worn extravagant Sotho costumes; many had probably acquired their guns at the diamond diggings, where they would also have acquired items of European clothing.) There was only one main route to the summit, a steep zig-zag path protected by carefully constructed stone breastworks. The Colonial troops, underestimating their enemy as usual, made a rash assault in early April. They failed to penetrate the first line of defences, and retired with 22 dead. At the end of May a Phuthi foray caught a party of Cape Yeomanry unawares and killed 20 more in their tents.

At the beginning of June the Colonial forces prepared for another assault. Moorosi's Mountain was subjected to a heavy bombardment, although the attacking force lacked mortars or howitzers, and most of the shellfire was ineffective against the stone defences. On 5 June the second attack took place, only to be driven back like the first. Observers noted with chagrin that the Phuthi seemed to be unusually good shots, one albino in particular being a crack marksman. Whenever the Colonial forces moved into the open, the Phuthi unleashed a withering fire upon them. The failure of the second assault led to several months of siege and negotiation. The Phuthi would be allowed to surrender, but must expect long prison sentences. They refused.

The final assault took place just after midnight on 3 November. The Cape Mounted Rifles spear-headed the attack, and scaling ladders were brought up to overcome the obstacles. This time it was successful. The attackers overran the defences, scaled the cliffs, and drove across the summit. Many Phuthi threw themselves over the precipices in an attempt to escape, but Moorosi and 40 of his followers were killed.

He had held out for eight months, including the rigours of the Basotholand winter, when food was scarce. Three hundred men with guns had kept 800 white troops, with modern breech-loaders and artillery, and 1,500 Africans, at bay: proof, were it needed, of the effectiveness of Sotho strategy.

Sekhukhune

While the southern Sotho coalesced around the leadership of Moshoeshoe, Sotho groups in the eastern Transvaal were increasingly dominated by the Pedi kingdom. The Pedi, under the chiefs of the dominant Maroteng clan, emerged as a powerful factor in the aftermath of the *mfecane*, and by the mid-19th century had built up a state organised along broadly similar lines to the Basotho—a central core of clans directly under the control of the king, and a number of allied chieftainships on the periphery. So powerful did the Pedi become that, during the reign of King Sekhukhune (1861–79) one observer commented that the chief 'enjoyed a fame as a chief of dignity and importance hardly inferior to the fame of Cetshwayo among the Zulus'. The Pedi certainly bested both early Boer expeditions, and the warriors of the other important local power, the Swazi. It was to take a major effort

by the Transvaal and two British campaigns before the Pedi were overthrown.

The origins of the conflict lay, as usual, in the question of disputed land. As the Transvaal filled up with whites, so there was competition for land on the Pedi borders. The existence of the Pedi kingdom made it difficult for the Transvaal to tax its own African population—malcontents simply placed themselves under Sekhukhune's protection. In their turn, the Pedi complained that their migrant workers were harassed and robbed when they travelled through the Transvaal on their way to the Cape and Natal. In the 1870s several chiefs, with or without Sekhukhune's permission, moved away from the Pedi heartland and settled close to Boer villages, fuelling fears of Pedi expansion. In 1876 the Transvaal attempted to overthrow the Pedi power-base: and a large Boer commando, supported by Swazi regiments, took to the field.

The Pedi army was organised along southern Sotho lines—age-regiments directly under the control of the king, with supporting contingents from allied chiefs. They may originally have been armed and dressed as other Sotho, but they soon

Chief Sekhukhune of the Pedi (in cloak) and members of his family photographed in Pretoria after their capture in December 1879. (Bryan Maggs)

The final assault on the Pedi capital Tsate, 28 November 1879. The town itself is protected by hills behind it and the solitary 'Fighting Kop' in front. Note British troops on the heights in the foreground and on the plain. (Author's collection)

acquired guns in large numbers. In the early 1860s, even before the discovery of diamonds, gangs of as many as 200 Pedi at a time, perhaps selected on a regimental basis, made the long journey to the southern Colonies to work for whites. On the return journey they would trade their pay for firearms. In 1862 a missionary working amongst the Pedi calculated that the army, fully mobilised, comprised about 12,000 warriors, of whom more than a third had guns. These would have been the usual poor-quality trade muskets; but the increased availability of more modern weapons which accompanied the discovery of diamonds gave the Pedi a chance to re-arm. By 1876 most of the warriors were armed with guns, the majority with breech-loaders. Unlike Moshoeshoe's Basotho, however, they did not adopt horses.

The 1876 campaign was a disaster for the Transvaal. The Pedi took to their mountain strongholds in true Sotho style, and the Boers showed a distinct reluctance to face them. The bulk of the fighting was left to the Swazi allies, who became disgruntled when it was clear that they were not supported, and who abandoned the campaign in disgust. The Boers fell back and built two forts on the fringes of Pedi territory, from which they attempted to raid and destroy Pedi crops to starve Sekhukhune into submission. Desultory skirmishing dragged on.

In 1877 Britain annexed the Transvaal as part of her Confederation scheme; and with it she inherited the Pedi problem. If the independence of the Zulu kingdom was seen as a barrier to the peaceful uniting of southern Africa, the existence of the Pedi was hardly less so; Colonial officials decided to pursue the war against Sekhukhune. In October 1878 the first British expedition against the Pedi set out under the command of Col. Hugh Rowlands.

Consisting of only 130 infantry and 338 mounted men, it was faced with a gruelling march through the Leolu Mountains to Tsate, Sekhukhune's capital. The Pedi employed tactics of harassment and ambush. It soon became clear that the force was hopelessly inadequate. A prolonged drought had led to shortage of water and forage, and horse-sickness broke out. Rowlands had little choice but to retreat.

The outbreak of the Zulu War prevented further British incursions until late in 1879. Having supervised the destruction of the Zulu kingdom the

Chief Langalibalele of the Hlubi and seven of his sons, photographed in Pietermaritzburg jail before their trial. (Killie Campbell Library)

British were in no mood to allow Sekhukhune free reign, however, and in September 1879 Sir Garnet Wolseley organised two columns—one comprising 400 soldiers and volunteers, 5,000–8,000 Swazis and 400 Transvaal Africans, the other 3,000 Europeans and 2,500 Africans—to converge on Tsate. The Pedi skirmished before Wolseley's advance, and fell back on Tsate.

Sekhukhune's capital was situated at the end of a long valley, nestling at the base of a line of hills. Directly in front of it lay a solitary hill which the Pedi had made into a stronghold. About 150 feet high, it was pitted with caves and covered with boulders, which had been reinforced with stone breastworks. It became known as *Ntswaneng*, the 'Fighting Kop'. The pressures of three years of war had reduced the Pedi strength considerably, and many allied chiefs no doubt kept warriors back in their own districts for fear of the Swazi. Tsate was defended by as few as 4,000 men; they were, however, both well entrenched and well armed.

Wolseley's attack took place at dawn on 28 November. After a stiff preliminary bombardment troops assaulted the Kop; but, while they carried the first line of breastworks, they were pinned down by heavy Pedi fire. At 9.30 a.m., however, the Swazis, who had approached from a different direction, appeared over the crest of the hills behind Tsate and stormed through the town. The Pedi put up stiff resistance, but had not expected an attack from the rear, and were overrun. A renewed attack was made on the Fighting Kop from all four sides, and after severe fighting it was carried; but many of the Pedi remained hidden in caves, and could not be driven out. Gun-cotton was used to blow up the breastworks in an attempt to frighten them into submission. It failed; on a number of occasions Pedi successfully cut the fuses. As night fell, it was decided to starve the defenders out. However, many Pedi took advantage of the cover of a heavy rainstorm to sally forth, burst through the picket, and escape.

As many as a thousand Pedi fell in the battle for Tsate, and the survivors were scattered. The Swazis were allowed to rampage unchecked through the kingdom for ten days. Sekhukhune himself had taken refuge in a cave behind the town; tracked down and captured on 2 December, he was sent into exile. Wolseley's campaign had thoroughly and effectively broken the power of the Pedi.

The Tswana

The discovery of diamonds near Kimberley had profound repercussions for the whole of southern Africa, not least on the people living in the immediate vicinity. The diamonds were actually discovered in an area known as Griqualand West, beyond the Orange River, the northern frontier of the Cape Colony. The Griqua were descendants of displaced Khoi from the Cape; but their settlements were small, and the majority of the population were Tswana Africans whose territory, Bechuanaland, lay beyond the Griqua borders.

Britain had shown a marked reluctance to become involved in Griqua affairs; but the discovery of diamonds shifted the economic balance, and Britain persuaded the Griqua to pass over their authority to the Crown, thus under-cutting a rival claim by the Orange Free State. This did little for the local Tswana, however, whose lifestyle was disrupted by the influx of white diggers in the diamond rushes from 1869; the prospectors' settlements were particularly anarchic. Complaints of mistreatment of Africans, shady land deals and exploitation led to outbreaks of violence.

In May 1878 a group of Tswana killed a storekeeper whom they believed to be implicated in unjust cattle confiscation; they then fled across the Griqua border into Bechuanaland, with a column of Colonial troops in pursuit. The rebels took up a position at the town of Dithakong, which was commanded by a low ridge covered with circular stone walls, the ruins of a settlement dating back to the 16th century. Here, on 24 July 1878, they were attacked by 300 troops under Col. W. O. Lanyon. After a three-hour bombardment the troops stormed the ridge. The Tswana put up a stiff resistance, but at the last minute broke and fled.

The battle of Dithakong was the last major action in the 1878 campaign, and Tswana resistance soon collapsed. White interest in the area increased in the 1880s, however, with a resulting disruption of the Tswana. Independent Bechuanaland was subject to pressure from both British commercial interests, and the Transvaal, whose Boer farmers were seeking a means of expanding westward. The European parties allied themselves to rival Tswana groups, who were already in competition for shrinking grazing land. The result was a series of inter-clan wars in which Boer freebooters hired themselves out as mercenaries in return for promises of land. Britain considered this situation unacceptable, and stepped in to refute the Transvaal's claims.

In 1885 an expedition under Sir Charles Warren occupied southern Bechuanaland without fighting, and it was annexed as British Bechuanaland. For the Tswana the main effect was to bring in Colonial land policies, which restricted them to 'native reserves'. This provoked a simmering discontent which erupted into violence following the outbreak of the cattle-disease rinderpest. White officials shot cattle to prevent the spread of the disease, but the inhabitants of the town of Phokwani felt that their cattle were killed rather than those of white farmers. Phokwani's rising was brief, and ruthlessly suppressed. The town was bombarded and razed to the ground in December 1896. Most of the survivors were captured, but some fled to the Langeberg

A naïf early artist's impression of the skirmish at Bushman's Pass, 4 November 1873, between Hlubi warriors of Chief Langalibalele and Colonial volunteers. The volunteers attempted to prevent the Hlubi from ascending the Pass, but firing broke out and three volunteers and two African auxiliaries were killed. (Killie Campbell Library)

Mountains in the west, where a rebel force was gathered under Chief Luka Jantje of the Tlhaping Tswana, a veteran of the 1878 campaign who was bitterly opposed to the whites. Between February and August 1897 about 4,000 Tswana men, women and children were besieged in the Langeberg by 2,000 Colonial troops. Luka proved an excellent hit-and-run leader, but his troops could not resist the combined Colonial assault which took place at the stronghold of Gamasep on 30 July 1897. The Tswana were overrun, and Luka himself killed leading a final desperate rush. His death marked the collapse of Tswana resistance.

The Tswana were a western branch of the Sotho, and their armies were traditionally organised along age-regiment lines. A sketch of Tlhaping warriors in the 1820s shows them wearing a costume similar to that of the southern Sotho—a breech-hide, a cloak of animal skin, and a ball of ostrich feathers on the head. Their shields, however, were squared off more

An Ndebele ('Matabele') war dance, sketched in the 1860s. At this stage Ndebele dress retained many Zulu features: these warriors wear otterskin headbands and ostrich plumes. Some appear to have ostrich feather shoulder capes, while others have Zulu-style cow-tail necklaces. (Author's collection)

than the Basotho type, with less prominent wings. Their weapons were spears and clubs.

By the 1870s, however, the Tswana were mostly armed with guns, and photos of captured rebels in 1897 show them to be wearing European clothing. Firearms had been exported to the Tswana by white entrepreneurs from the 1860s, to stimulate the valuable Khalahari hunting industry. In just one year, 1872, when the trade was at its height, no less than 7,902 guns, 106,650 lb of powder, 246,800 lb of lead, and 2,249,000 percussion caps were *legally* sold to the Tswana—and doubtless many more illegally. After Phokwani, an examination of captured guns revealed that most were Enfields, with a number of Martini-Henry carbines.

Throughout the wars, Tswana forces were small. In one of the 1878 battles a Colonial column was attacked by '200 footmen and 40 horsemen armed with guns'. In the more serious 1897 war between 1,200 and 1,500 Tswana were killed, and 3,800 men, women and children taken prisoner. Many of these were doubtless non-combatants; in individual battles, the Tswana forces numbered hundreds rather than thousands.

Natal

The British first came to Natal in 1824, in the shape of a group of adventurers and ivory hunters who managed to persuade the Zulu king Shaka to grant them rights to Port Natal, the best harbour in the region. At that time the *mfecane* was at its height, and Natal had been largely depopulated by Zulu raids. However, as the white presence grew the country filled up once more with Africans, who placed themselves under European protection. For a short period at the end of the 1830s Natal was occupied by Boer Trekkers; but in 1842 British troops drove them out, and in 1843 Britain annexed Natal.

The two main concerns for the British administration regarding African policy were the presence of the independent Zulu kingdom north of the Tugela River, and the influx of Africans into Natal. These latter were both survivors of Shaka's raids, returning to claim their old lands, and political refugees from Zululand seeking asylum. In the early days of the Colony the government was far too weak to challenge the might of the Zulu; but attempts were made to restrict Natal Africans to reserves, known as 'locations', so that the remainder of the Colony could be made available to white farmers.

In 1848 the Hlubi clan, about 7,000 strong under their chief Langalibalele, broke away from Zululand and fled to Natal. The Hlubi had been powerful marauders during the *mfecane*, but a series of defeats had weakened their strength, and they had been incorporated as vassals into the Zulu kingdom. Langalibalele had patiently rebuilt the Hlubi, but had fallen foul of the Zulu king Mpande, and had fled under threat of a Zulu attack. The Natal authorities were powerless to prevent such an influx, but they did their best to restrict the Hlubi to a location in the foothills of the Drakensberg.

Here, for 20 years, Langalibalele lived a largely independent life, with the minimum of interference from the government. Along with several other intact clans who settled in Natal territory, he was given permission to hold the annual *umkhosi*, or First Fruits festival, and to raise *amabutho* age-regiments. It is not clear whether these regiments wore distinctive uniforms, after the manner of their Zulu counterparts, or whether they carried full-size war-

The dawn attack on the British South Africa Company's laager at Shangani, 25 October 1893—the first major action of the 1893 Ndebele War. (Author's collection)

shields. They may have worn ceremonial costumes at the *umkhosi* ceremonies, but there are no references to uniforms in the subsequent fighting, and it seems probable that the warriors would have carried the small shields that were used for everyday protection. The warriors lived among their families, and only mustered when the chief needed the services of a particular regiment. Although in the days before the *mfecane* Hlubi men wore a Sotho-style breech-hide, and a distinctive braided hairstyle known as the *iziyendane* instead of the *isicoco* headring, by this time prolonged contact had made their dress indistinguishable from the Zulu. The *iziyendane* hairstyle was still fashionable among some young men, however.

Like many other African groups the Hlubi sent their men to work on the diamond-fields, and they returned home armed with guns. This was to be their downfall. In 1872 the Natal government became seriously alarmed at the number of guns filtering into the Colony's black population and in March 1873 Langalibalele was ordered to give up all unregistered firearms among his people. It seems likely that at first the chief did not think this a very important matter; the government most certainly did, however, and had decided to make an example of the Hlubi. Messages between the authorities and Langalibalele became increasingly heated, and the Hlubi became seriously alarmed that their chief was about to be attacked. The young men of the chiefdom naturally refused to give up their arms. The *amabutho* mustered in a state of increasing tension. The Colony called out its volunteers.

At the last minute, the chief baulked at the

prospect of an open conflict with the whites. He decided to flee: the chiefdom had used such a strategy successfully in 1848—it was worth trying again. Behind the Hlubi lay the Drakensberg Mountains, but the high Bushman's Pass led over the escarpment and into the uninhabited plateau of east Basotholand. On 3 November 1873 Langalibalele rode across the mountains, and the next day the Hlubi followed him.

The government moved to cut them off. A small party of volunteers under the command of Maj. Anthony Durnford, RE, ascended the Drakensberg by a different route, and rode round to block Bushman's Pass. By the time they arrived the Hlubi were already approaching the Pass. Durnford's orders were not to fire the first shot, but as the young Hlubi warriors pressed around his line a skirmish broke out. Three volunteers and two African levies were killed, and Durnford himself was badly

wounded in the arm. The volunteers retreated in disorder, and the Hlubi made their escape.

The Bushman's Pass affair was only a skirmish, but it sent shock-waves through white Natal. It seemed to justify latent settler fears of African uprisings. The government response was ruthless. Two companies of regular troops, with Colonial volunteers and African levies, marched through the Hlubi location, destroying huts and rounding up any cattle that remained. Any stragglers who resisted were shot. Within a few weeks the Hlubi chiefdom in Natal ceased to exist.

Langalibalele himself realised that further struggle was futile, and surrendered to the authorities in Basotholand. Some of his young warriors refused to submit, and Colonial patrols dispersed them. The chief himself was put on trial, and after farcical proceedings was found guilty of treason and rebellion, and exiled to Cape Town. Within a few years he would be joined by the erstwhile leader of the most powerful black state in southern Africa, the deposed king Cetshwayo kaMpande. In 1879 Britain finally broke the power of the Zulu state[1].

An Ndebele chief, wearing a leopardskin cloak indicative of his rank. The Ndebele headring, marking the status of a married man, was smaller than the Zulu original, and worn further forward on the head. (Bryan Maggs)

Zimbabwe

In 1890 Cecil Rhodes, the diamond magnate, financed the occupation of Mashonaland, part of modern Zimbabwe, by the troops of his British South Africa Company. Rhodes' motives were two-fold: he hoped that Mashonaland might prove to contain the same mineral resources as had been found a decade earlier in the Transvaal; and he also hoped that by completing the encirclement of the Transvaal with British possessions, he would force the Boer republic to accept greater outside influence.

The dominant power in Zimbabwe in 1890 was the Ndebele kingdom. In the 1820s Chief Mzilikazi kaMashobane of the Khumalo clan, which was incorporated as an ally into the Zulu state of King Shaka, broke away and led a handful of followers over the Drakensberg and into the interior. This

[1]Full details of the Zulu military system and the war of 1879 have not been given here, as they can be found in Elite 21, *The Zulus* by Ian Knight, and Men-at-Arms 57, *The Zulu War* by Angus McBride, both illustrated in colour by Angus McBride.

Cape Frontier Wars, mid-19th C:
1,2: Xhosa warriors
  3: Chief Maqoma, c.1835
  4: Cape Mounted Rifles renegade, c.1852

4

A

Cape Frontier Wars, 1870s:
1: Ngqika warrior
2: Chief Sandile, 1878
3: Gcaleka warrior

B

Basotho warriors:
1: Warrior, first half 19th C.
2: Chief, c.1850
3: Warrior, Gun War, 1880

C

1: Hlubi warrior, Langalibalele Rebellion, 1873
2: Zulu warrior, Nokhenkhe regiment, 1879
3: Pedi warrior, Sekhukhune campaign, 1879

D

Ndebele warriors muster in ceremonial regalia, c.1893:
1: Ndoda – senior warrior
2: Ijaha – junior warrior – of Insuga regiment
3: Warrior, Imbizo regiment

1   2   3

E

F   1: Ndbele warrior, Holi caste   2: Ndbele warrior, war dress, 1893-96   3: Rebel, 1896-97

The Boers:
1: Voortrekker, c.1842, with cannon *Ou Grietje*
2: Commandant Andries Pretorius, c.1838
3: Volunteer, 1881

The Anglo-Boer War:
1: Boer commandant, 1899
2: Gunner, Transvaal Staats Artillerie
3: Commando volunteer, 1899-1902
4: 'Bitter-ender', 1902

band was one of those which so devastated the Sotho. The Sotho called Mzilikazi's followers *Matabele*, a name which seems to have referred to their habit of ducking down behind their large war-shields. The marauders adopted this name for themselves in its Nguni form, *Ndebele*.

Mzilikazi established a small kingdom for himself in the Transvaal, until the arrival of the Boer Voortrekkers led to a war which drove the Ndebele out. Eventually they crossed the Limpopo and settled in Zimbabwe. This area was already populated by African peoples known collectively as Mashona. Victorian propaganda suggested that the Ndebele were ruthless conquerors who slaughtered the Mashona for sport, but the truth was a more complex relationship in which some Mashona were absorbed into the Ndebele state, while others paid tribute or formed alliances. Nevertheless, the Ndebele state was characterised by a three-tier class-system in which the élite, descendants of those from Zululand, were called *Zansi*; Sotho from the Transvaal, *Enhla*, 'those from along the way'; and the Mashona, *Holi*, a term of contempt.

The Ndebele army was organised along the Zulu pattern, adapted to the nation's particular conditions. It was organised into *amabutho* age-regiments. By the 1870s, however, when Mzilikazi's son Lobengula was on the throne, the *amabutho* do not seem to have been formed regularly, but usually in response to times of national crisis. When a regiment was formed, the king would instruct it to build a regimental barracks. The warriors would congregate at this barracks throughout the period of the regiment's direct service, a matter of a few years, after which time its members would be allowed to establish personal homesteads in the same region. Generally, the king controlled the pace at which the regiments married. In the Zulu system this marked the point at which the warriors ceased to be directly under the king's control; the Ndebele version seems to have involved less severe restrictions, however, individual warriors marrying while still living in regimental barracks. When the regiment dispersed it continued to dominate the area, and the *amabutho* system was thus part of a process of internal colonisation.

When subsequent generations reached maturity they might be formed into a new regiment, or used to reinforce that of their fathers. Some attempts

The battle of Bembesi, Ndebele War, 1 November 1893: the Imbizo and Ingubo regiments make their fateful charge on the Company laager. (Author's collection)

were made to recruit on a class basis, regiments with a high proportion of Zansi warriors being regarded as the best material. Regiments consisting entirely of Holi were formed from subject chiefdoms, or from Holi attached to Ndebele settlements as domestic servants. Some sources put Lobengula's army as high as 38 regiments, a total of 15,000 men, in 1893; some of these were probably sections of regiments, but in any case most Ndebele *amabutho* were much smaller than their Zulu equivalents, with between 200 and 500 warriors apiece. Only regiments which enjoyed a high degree of royal patronage—e.g. Imbizo, the first regiment formed by Lobengula, or the young and arrogant Insuga—might approach a strength of 1,000.

Costume and Weapons

Initially, the Ndebele regiments were dressed in the style of their Zulu counterparts. Descriptions of them in the Transvaal show that they were wearing Zulu-style loin coverings, cow-tails around the arms and legs and suspended over the chest and back, and headbands of otterskin with a variety of different plumes. The availability or otherwise of different feathers and furs meant that by the 1890s the Ndebele were wearing a costume uniquely their own. The Zulu-style loin-covering, a belt of hide around the waist with strips of fur hanging down the front and a square of hide over the buttocks, remained the basic pattern, although jackal-skin was often used at the front. A breech-hide was also common, with a single piece of skin being passed between the legs and suspended front and back from the belt. Elite regiments wore a kilt over this. This was based on the Zulu kilt, but the original pelts were not available in Zimbabwe, and the

An Ndebele *ijaha*, or young warrior, in characteristic ostrich feather headdress and cape, c.1893. The shield is in the Zulu style, but his waist-kilt is poorly constructed compared with Zulu models. (Zimbabwe National Archives)

Ndebele kilt was usually made of twisted strips of cat or monkey-skin, with a resulting loss of quality.

The Zulu distinction between married and unmarried men persisted in the Ndebele division between *amadoda*, older men, and *amajaha*, young warriors. The dress of the *amadoda* consisted of a stuffed headband of otterskin, with single crane feathers worn at either side or at the front of the head. By definition, however, the numbers of the *amadoda* were few, and most Ndebele warriors wore the uniform of the *amajaha*. This consisted of a circlet of black ostrich feathers worn around the head, and a large clipped pompon of the same over the forehead. A cape, also of black ostrich feathers, was worn around the shoulders. Regimental distinctions seem to have been confined to additional plumes stitched into the pompon. The Imbizo regiment, for example, is thought to have worn a single long white ostrich feather in its headdress. The other main regimental distinction was the colour of the

hair left on the front of the war-shields. This followed the Zulu pattern, with senior regiments carrying predominantly white shields, and junior ones black shields. There is, unfortunately, little specific evidence relating to Lobengula's *amabutho*, but the Imbizo may have carried white shields with black spots, and the Insuga black shields with white spots. The Holi regiments were probably poorly dressed by comparison with the Zansi. Like the Zulu, the Ndebele did not wear all their finery into battle, although the pompon does seem to have been retained.

Ndebele armament had also declined since the Zululand days. War shields were smaller, and less well made; the binding which held the stick to the hide was often weaker and less neat. Weapons comprised stabbing and throwing spears. It has been suggested that when the Ndebele migrated they cut themselves off from their traditional sources of ironwork, and that in Zimbabwe most smiths were Mashona. Be this as it may, Ndebele spears were both smaller and cruder than their Zulu equivalents. It is possible that original spears forged in Zululand during the *mfecane* were still in use in 1893, much reduced by constant regrinding. The Ndebele stabbing spear had a blade about 12 in. long. Both clubs and axes were occasionally carried.

Being on the fringes of the area affected by the gold and diamond rushes, the Ndebele were not as well armed with guns as other groups. Nonetheless, Lobengula amassed a number of percussion rifles which he distributed amongst the *amabutho*. In addition, part of the price paid by Rhodes to occupy Mashonaland was 1,000 Martini-Henry rifles. Without training, however, the Ndebele warriors were to prove unable to put these to good effect.

The 1893 Campaign

Rhodes' column occupied Mashonaland, to the east of the main Ndebele settlements, without fighting. However, there can be little doubt that his real intention was to occupy the whole of Zimbabwe, and the interests of the Company's settlers and prospectors were at variance with those of their independent African neighbour. In 1893 Rhodes invaded Ndebeleland; two columns advanced together from Mashonaland, and a third advanced from the south. Lobengula's response was to instruct those regiments occupying the southern districts to oppose that column, and to unleash his main striking arm against those coming from the east.

The first battle took place on the banks of the Shangani River at dawn on 25 October 1893. Rhodes' columns were small, a combined force of no more than 700 mounted volunteers and a number of African allies, but they were well armed with Maxim guns and artillery. The two columns had camped side by side, and formed a linked laager or defensive wagon-circle. The Ndebele, 3,500 strong, surrounded the laager during the night, and had planned a co-ordinated attack at dawn; but their presence was discovered, and the attack began prematurely. A heavy fire was poured on the laager, which replied with Maxim fire that scythed down the Ndebele rushes. Repeated charges were repulsed with heavy casualties. At last, having sustained 500 or 600 casualties, the Ndebele withdrew. The Company columns continued their advance the same day.

On 1 November the Ndebele attacked again at Bembesi. This time the *impi* was stronger: 6,000 men, reinforced with Lobengula's reserve, the Imbizo and Ingubu regiments. As many as 2,000 men were estimated to be armed with rifles. Once more, however, the attack was premature and unco-ordinated, this time in broad daylight. The result was catastrophic: the Imbizo and Ingubu put in a charge which melted before the Maxims, 100 yards from the laagers; it is thought that as many as 40 per cent of the two regiments were mown down. The Ndebele were shocked and disheartened, and drifted from the field. A few days later Rhodes' columns occupied Lobengula's capital, Bulawayo. The southern column came in shortly after; it had been attacked once on the march, but had easily driven the attackers off.

King Lobengula himself had fled on hearing the news of Bembesi. Rhodes' main concern was to parcel out the conquered territory among his volunteers, but, almost as an after-thought, he did organise a column to pursue the king. The Company's confidence was premature; the Ndebele were defeated but not broken. As the column marched north towards the Shangani River, it encountered large numbers of Ndebele warriors, still loyal to Lobengula. On the night of 3 December 1893, a patrol of 30 men was sent across the Shangani River to locate Lobengula. They were trapped by heavy rain which made the return crossing impractical. The *amabutho* turned, and massacred them to a man. The column began a dismal retreat, harried for much of the way by the Ndebele.

It was the only Ndebele victory in the war of 1893. The king contracted smallpox and died in January 1894. Ndebeleland and Mashonaland became united as Rhodesia. The *amabutho* had gone to war in fine style, but their frontal assaults, after the method of their Zulu forebears, had proved disastrously inadequate in the face of the Company's Maxims. At Shangani and Bembesi the Ndebele had wasted the potential of their own firepower. The lesson had been learned the hard way, and in their last victory the Ndebele had picked off members of the pursuing patrol with rifle fire before overwhelming them in a rush. But then, the patrol had no Maxims.

Rhodes' over-confidence continued in the years

Two young Ndebele warriors in the 1896 rebellion. These are probably 'friendlies' who sided with the whites, but the appearance of rebels would not have been markedly different. (Zimbabwe National Archives)

Ndebele *izinduna*, photographed during the peace negotiations to end the 1896 rebellion. (Author's collection)

after the Ndebele War. In fact, many of the regimental settlements in the outlying areas had not been touched by the campaign, and remained viable military units. Once it became clear that the European occupation was permanent, not a temporary raid of the type the Ndebele themselves practised, the African population became increasingly unsettled. They were further disturbed by heavy-handed Company officials attempting to collect taxes and to force them to work for whites, and by natural catastrophes, such as the cattle disease rinderpest, which wiped out their herds. In March 1896, taking advantage of the absence of large numbers of the Company's troops on the ill-fated Jameson Raid, the Ndebele rose in revolt.

The 1896 Rising

The organisation of the revolt is the subject of some controversy, though it seems likely that it had much to do with an attempt to revive the old Ndebele state. Certainly a son of Lobengula was championed as his heir, and many of the leaders were *izinduna* from the old days. Those *amabutho* which had not been broken in 1893 took the field as military units. Some may even have worn their old regimental uniforms, though the majority of the rebels wore minimal regalia.

In the early days of the uprising, the rebels massacred whites in the outlying districts, and forced the Europeans to take refuge in laagered settlements. Rhodes' capital, built on the ruins of Bulawayo, was besieged by rebels who took up a position along the natural barrier of the Umguza River north of the town. Several patrols sent out to dislodge them met with little success. The rebels were not, however, able to completely isolate the town, nor were they in a position to overrun its defences. When Rhodes organised relief columns the Ndebele were forced onto the defensive. The majority retreated to the boulder-strewn kopjes of the Matapo Hills south of Bulawayo, from which it proved difficult to dislodge them. To make matters worse from the Company point of view, in June the Mashona rose in revolt.

The Company had always been contemptuous of Mashona fighting capabilities, and, indeed, had regarded themselves as liberators of the Mashona from the Ndebele yoke. It came as a profound shock, therefore, when several Mashona chiefs unleashed their followers against white farms and mines. The majority of these chiefs were old allies or vassals of the Ndebele, and seem to have been drawn into the revolt to support their Ndebele colleagues. The Mashona lacked the centralised military tradition of the Ndebele, each chief commanding his own warriors. After the initial raids the chiefs retreated to their individual strongholds, fortified kopjes which had been tested in the unsettled tribal years. The Company was forced to undertake a long and wearying campaign of suppression. It was August 1896 before the Ndebele, after protracted negotiation with Rhodes himself, agreed to surrender, and the Mashona remained under arms until October 1897.

Generally, the Ndebele performance in 1896 had been better than in 1893. The military commanders had a more appropriate understanding of tactical realities; massed charges were abandoned in favour of ambushes, short rushes and harassing tactics. Much more effective use was made of rifles. In defence, both Ndebele and Shona took full advantage of natural cover, and stuck tenaciously to a series of strongholds. This greatly reduced the effectiveness of the Company's artillery and Maxims, and the battles in the Mambo and Matopo Hills were fought amongst the boulders by foot-soldiers on both sides.

'A Gallant Deed': Lt. Crewe, Grey's Scouts, covering the escape of a wounded colleague during one of the actions on the Umguza River, 1896. The appearance of the rebels is typical. (Durban Art Gallery)

The Boers

The prolonged conflict between the British Empire and the Boers was the result of a profound difference of outlook between the two white groups in southern Africa. The Boers were tough, independent frontier farmers who regarded themselves as white Africans, appointed to a unique rôle on the continent by God. They bitterly resented the bureaucratic authority of a British Colonial regime which sought to deal even-handedly with Africans. As early as 1819 there was a minor Boer uprising, followed by a botched execution, a reaction to unsympathetic British taxation policies. In 1833 Britain abolished slavery within her dominions; and this, coupled with poor compensation to slave owners, and new laws regulating the exploitation of African labour, seemed to strike at the foundations of the Boer way of life. In the Great Trek which followed some 12,000 Boer men, women and children emigrated from British Colonial territory, and attempted to establish their own states in the interior.

Britain regarded the Trek Boers as British citizens, but made little attempt to stop the migration, trusting to the hardships of the African landscape to curb the movement. However, the Boers encountered several of the African kingdoms which had emerged a decade before from the *mfecane*, and the resulting wars threatened to upset British policy towards Africans on the Cape borders. In 1838 the Boers fought a particularly bloody war against the Zulus, and established a republic in Natal. Subsequent attempts by the Boers to relocate Africans within Natal led to Britain asserting her rights to Natal, a claim which had its origins in a land-grant awarded to British adventurers by the Zulu king Shaka.

In 1842 two companies of the 27th Regiment under the command of Maj. T. C. Smith marched up from the Cape to seize Port Natal, the most viable harbour in the area. Smith built a makeshift fort, and opened negotiations with the Boer leader

Pretorius' Trekkers line the mangrove trees at Port Natal, waiting to ambush Capt. Smith's column on the beach beyond: the battle of Congella, 23 May 1842. The short jackets and powder horns worn by the Boers are clear even in this pencil sketch. (Killie Campbell Library)

Andries Pretorius, the man who defeated the Zulus. Having come thus far to escape the British, Pretorius was in no mood to accept Smith's authority. Smith decided to attack him, and on the night of 23 May marched part of his force along the beach to attack the Boer camp. The Boers discovered the movement and ambushed Smith's column, which was driven back to the fort with heavy casualties. For a month Smith was besieged in his fort, until British reinforcements arrived by sea and drove the Boers off. Britain annexed Natal the next year, and many Boers were so disgruntled that they crossed back over the Drakensberg and into the interior.

Even here they were not free of British influence. In 1845 Boers living beyond the Orange River were in dispute with local Griqua. The Griqua claimed allegiance to the Crown, and a British force was sent to intervene. In April it met a Boer commando at Zwartkopjes, and, after a stiff fight, the Boers were driven from the field. British influence beyond the Orange was stepped up, and in 1848 Governor Sir Harry Smith annexed the area as the Orange River Sovereignty. Those Boers who objected appealed to Andries Pretorius, now in the Transvaal, who came down and organised a commando. Smith marched to confront the rebels and met them at Boomplaats on 29 August. The Boers occupied a low ridge across the road, but Smith's assault was so rapid and well co-ordinated that he rolled up their line and forced them to retreat. The uprising collapsed but Smith's triumph was short-lived. The continual fighting against Boers, Xhosa and Basotho, with its

inevitable expense, was unacceptable to the home government, and Britain renounced rights to land beyond the Orange, accepting the independence of the Orange Free State and the Transvaal.

The continued difficulties of the southern African situation led to a reversal of this policy in the 1870s. At that time, the Transvaal Republic was administratively and financially in harsh straits, and held to be in danger from the Zulu and Pedi states. In 1877 Britain annexed the Transvaal, with the aquiescence of some of the Boer leaders. Small British garrisons were established across the country, and British troops suppressed the Pedi and Zulu. The majority of Transvaalers were opposed to annexation, however, and once the African threat had been removed the Transvaal rebelled. A British column en route for the capital, Pretoria, was cut to pieces by long-range rifle fire at Bronkhorst Spruit in December 1880, and the British garrisons were besieged.

In the subsequent fighting, the Transvaal forces were completely successful. The British commander, Gen. Sir George Colley, mustered a force in Natal and set off to relieve the besieged garrisons. The Boers blocked his path at the Drakensberg pass of Laing's Nek. On 28 January 1881 Colley made a frontal assault on the Boer lines. His men, wearing the scarlet tunics and white helmets of the Zulu war, were met by heavy Boer fire, and the attack failed. While Colley waited for reinforcements, the Boers moved down from the mountains to threaten his line of communication. Colley marched out to confront them at the Ingogo River on 8 February, but once more his force was caught in the open and pinned down by Boer marksmanship. Only an orderly retreat under cover of darkness allowed Colley to extricate his force. On 27 February, he occupied Majuba, a tall, flat-topped mountain which overlooked the Boer camps behind Laing's Nek, and seemed to command their position. In fact, Majuba proved a death trap once the Boers discovered the British presence and counter-attacked. British troops silhouetted against the skyline were easily picked off. The Boers overran the summit, and Colley was killed.

The disaster at Majuba brought the Transvaal War to a close. Britain abandoned the Transvaal, retaining only a vague claim to suzerainity. It was not long, however, before the discovery of gold in

1885 re-awakened Imperial interest. Large numbers of miners, chiefly of British descent, flooded into the Republic, and became the subject of a heated debate over enfranchisement. The Boers, led by Paul Kruger, who had been a leading opponent of annexation a decade before, refused to grant rights to outsiders who might give over the Transvaal to British interests. In 1895 Cecil Rhodes tried to force the issue by provoking a capitalist coup; troops from Rhodes' British South Africa Company, under the command of Dr L. S. Jameson, rode down from Rhodesia to support a miners' uprising. But the uprising failed to materialise, and Jameson was defeated by the Boers at Doornkop on 2 January 1896. The failure of the Jameson Raid led to the Transvaal stepping up preparations for war. After the collapse of protracted negotiations, the Transvaal declared war on Britain in October 1899. The Orange Free State rallied to the aid of her fellow republic.

A detailed account of the Anglo-Boer War is beyond the scope of a work such as this. Broadly, it fell into three phases: Boer invasions of British colonies, the British counter-attack, and a prolonged period of guerrilla warfare. The combined forces of the two republics numbered some 50,000 men, considerably more than the British troops garrisoning the Cape and Natal. The Boer plan was to strike swiftly and overwhelm the British before reinforcements could arrive. However, large numbers were wasted besieging British-held towns such as Kimberley and Mafeking in the west; and the advance into Natal bogged down in the long investment of Ladysmith. Initial British attempts to check these incursions met with disaster at Stormberg in the Cape, Magersfontein on the Kimberley front, and Colenso in Natal ('Black Week', December 1899). The heavy fighting at Spion Kop in Natal in January 1900 was bloody but inconclusive. In February the British went on to the

A Boer family at camp. With no regular army, Boer forces were an armed citizenry; during the days of the Trek, women and children often had to take part in the defence of wagon laagers, loading rifles for their menfolk. The wagon here is typical of the Trek period. Although this family was sketched in 1879, their appearance would have been much the same between the 1830s and 1880s. (Author's collection)

A group of Boers captured by a sortie from the besieged Pretoria garrison, 1881. (Bryan Maggs)

offensive. The Boers were seriously defeated at Paardeberg on the western front, and a series of actions forced a way through to Ladysmith. The Boers went on to the defensive, and in March the Free State capital of Bloemfontein fell. After a pause to receive heavy reinforcements, the British commander Lord Roberts advanced, and took the Transvaal capital Pretoria in early June.

The British expected this to end the war; but Kruger led his government into exile, and undefeated Boer commandos took to the countryside to wage a guerrilla war. Boer society was split into 'hands-uppers', who were prepared to surrender, and 'bitter-enders', determined to fight to the last. The British responded with a number of sweeps across hostile territory, then built lines of block-houses across the veld. To prevent guerrilla bands being supplied by Boer farms, Boer civilians were rounded up and placed in concentration camps and their farms destroyed. The cramped and insanitary conditions of the camps led to thousands of deaths from disease and malnutrition. Instead of sapping the Boer resolve, this increased their bitterness and determination to resist. It was not until May 1902 that the war of attrition forced the guerrilla leaders to surrender at Vereeniging.

Organisation

Boer armies throughout the 19th century were essentially citizens' militia, organised around the commando system. This system was seldom regularised, but its basic principles were understood by all. All males between the ages of about 16 and 60 within a particular district were subject to military service when called out by their local Field-Cornets, or Captains. Each man provided his own weapons, ammunition and horse, and provisions for the first few days. He would not normally expect to be paid, although the government would have some responsibilities for subsequent provisions. The first commando took to the field in 1715 to punish San raiders at the Cape, and the system became tried and tested in the unsettled conditions of the Cape Frontier. It provided Boer armies for the Trekker wars against both Africans and British, and persisted with only minor modifications through to the Anglo-Boer War.

At the start of that war, each commando, led by a Commandant, was divided into two or more Field-Cornetcies, which were supposed to consist of up to 200 men each, and each Field Cornetcy into Corporalships of about 25 men apiece. In fact the commandos varied greatly in size, the largest in 1899 being that from Potchefstroom, at 3,000, and the smallest from Springs with only 60. Each commando was run on a democratic basis, each

Boer having the right to vote for his officers and express his opinion on military matters. At the start of the war many Commandants were mature men whose rank was due to their status in civilian life. If they did not prove able leaders, however, their followers were free to join other commandos. As the war progressed, therefore, a new generation of skilled guerrilla leaders, such as Botha, De Wet and Smuts emerged. Such individual freedoms, anarchic by British standards, were a characteristic of the system. The French traveller Delagourge commented on the appearance of a commando in the 1838 Zulu campaign:

'(They were) scaling the hills helter-skelter, bearing their long guns ungracefully on their shoulders. From their commandant to the simple mounted man, there was no distinction in bearing, none in carrying out orders, which no one was tempted to give, because no one cared to obey, no mode of punishment existing'.

Tactics and Weapons

Military outlook was shaped by the realities of frontier life. A prolonged and costly campaign would oblige men to abandon their families and farms to the risk of natural disaster and African raids, and a small population could not support heavy casualties. The Boers therefore preferred to fight swift campaigns and, though they were tough, daring and courageous, their bravery was of a different order to the European professionals' 'fight to the last man' philosophy.

In wars against Africans tactics were simple. Transport was provided by pack-horse or ox-wagon, and these were used for defensive purposes in the wagon-circle or laager. A well-prepared laager had the pole of each wagon run under the one in front, the wagons linked by chains, and the gaps between the wheels sealed with thorn-bush or wooden gates. Such laagers were primarily intended for use against an enemy unarmed with firearms, but the habit of laagering camps continued through the Anglo-Boer War. In offence, the Boers were mounted infantrymen. Against Africans they would ride to within close range, dismount and open fire. Against the British they skirmished, making the most of natural cover. At Laing's Nek in 1881 they commanded the high ground, and took shelter in shallow trenches behind roughly constructed stone walls. This remained a characteristic tactic in the Boer War, modified on occasion to confuse British artillery by building false

A typical Boer group, Colesberg, February 1899. Note the modern bolt-action magazine rifles, and the variety of bandoliers. Hanging from the line are strips of sun-dried meat, *biltong*, a traditional food for Boers expecting to live without regular provisions. (National Army Museum)

Boer heavy artillery: a 'Long Tom' of the Transvaal Staats Artillerie, 1900. Most of the gunners are in uniform at this stage, although many took to wearing civilian clothes later. (National Army Museum)

trenches on heights to draw fire, but occupying forward trenches at the base of the feature. Until the Transvaal War, at least, the majority of Boers were natural horsemen, and the 'bitter-ender' commandos were ideally suited to the free-ranging hit-and-run tactics of 1900–02. Their mobility and knowledge of the ground enabled them to outrun British columns encumbered with supply trains.

In the early wars, most Boers were also good shots, experienced in handling their firearms throughout a life in which their survival might depend on their hunting skills. The Trekkers' firearms were a variety of flintlock and percussion smooth-bore civilian hunting guns, purchased according to taste and means. From the 1840s an expensive heavy-calibre double-barrelled elephant-gun known as a *roer* was highly prized. By the time of the 1881 war Westley-Richards breech-loading carbines were popular. Following the Jameson Raid, the Boer republics bought-in large numbers of modern Mauser magazine rifles, which were then re-sold to the commandos for a nominal sum. By this period more Boers who took to the field were from urban areas than ever before, with correspondingly less experience of practical shooting, so it may be suggested that the consistency of Boer marksmanship in 1899–1902 has been over-stated.

For artillery the Trekkers had a number of small ships' cannon, mounted on carriages improvised from wagon parts. These were used against Smith's fort at Port Natal in 1842, and several were apparently still in use in 1881. By 1899 both republics had professional artillery arms. The *Staats Artillerie van de O.V.S.* (Orange Free State) was established as early as 1857; in 1899 it was commanded by a German, Maj. Albrecht, and consisted of 400 men and 14×7.5cm Krupp guns. The *Staats Artillerie van de Z.A.R.* (South African Republic Transvaal) was founded in 1874, and began the Anglo-Boer War with 400 men, four 6in. Creusot ox-drawn guns, four 4.7in. Krupp howitzers, eight 2.95in. Krupp Quick-Firing guns, two Maxim Nordenfeldts and 22 1pdr. Maxims ('Pom-Poms'). In 1901, having lost its guns, it was re-organised as a mounted corps. Both units had dress uniforms of European style, but fought in drab fatigues when they wore uniforms at all. The Transvaal also boasted 1,200 ZARPs. (South African Republic Police), who possessed far more military discipline than the commandos.

Costume

A Boer in uniform was generally, however, a rare sight. Most fought in their everyday farming clothes, and these reflected in a general sense the fashions of the age. In the 1830s and '40s, short jackets and straw hats were common, with powder-horns attached to waist belts and haversacks for shot slung over the shoulder. In 1881 bandoliers were of the looped variety, to take single cartridges. By 1899 most bandoliers were of the type to take clips of bullets in flapped pouches. Trekker commandants favoured long dark coats and tall hats as symbols of their authority, and this habit continued in 1881 and into the early part of the Anglo-Boer War. Some Boers began that war with coloured ribbons or cockades in their hats, but this did not last. A number of foreign volunteer units, from Ireland, Europe and America, joined the Boer forces, but these had no distinguishing features apart from the occasional cockade. Once the rigours of the war of attrition began to bite, many 'bitter-enders' were reduced to dire straits, and were forced to replenish their supplies of weapons, ammunition and clothing from dead or captured British troops—despite a British directive that all Boers found wearing khaki would be shot as spies. (By the latter part of the war, at least, the conflict was prosecuted with considerable bitterness on both sides. For the British Army, fighting a counter-guerrilla war against European irregulars who drifted in and out of the cover of the civil population was a wholly new and unpleasant experience; and there were excesses on both sides.)

The Anglo-Boer War cost over 20,000 dead on each side, with tens of thousands more sick, wounded, and ruined. (More British and Dominion military horses died during this war than in the First World War.) It had meant hardship for countless black Africans, who were not directly involved but over whose heads it was fought. It marked the effective end of British military involvement in southern Africa; when the last Zulu uprising broke out in Natal in 1906 it was suppressed entirely by Colonial, rather than British regular troops.

It had taken just under a century for Britain to overcome her enemies and achieve her political aims. Ironically, the policy of reconstruction and reconciliation followed by the government in the aftermath of the Anglo-Boer War led to a decline in British political influence. Today, it is the descendants of the Trekkers who rule South Africa, having long since repudiated the last nominal links with Britain; and the legacy of past conflicts between Boers and Africans can still be discerned in the present troubles which disturb a rich and beautiful land.

The Plates

A1: Xhosa warrior, mid-19th century

A Xhosa warrior in typical traditional dress—naked except for a hide cloak held across the body for protection. The majority of ordinary Xhosa warriors would have worn this style of dress throughout the Cape Frontier Wars. Note the throwing spear with a sharpened metal prong instead of a blade.

A2: Xhosa warrior, mid-19th century

A young Xhosa warrior wearing a headdress of grey wing feathers. The exact significance of this headdress is uncertain, although it may have been worn by young initiates keen to demonstrate their prowess. It features in engravings depicting warriors as late as 1850. The shield is of a mid-19th century pattern; earlier shields were more oblong in shape. By this time shields in general were not

Improvised ways of carrying ammunition: a Boer waistcoat with pockets for cartridges, and a canvas bandolier. Anglo-Boer War, 1899–1902. (National Army Museum)

common, although isolated examples were taken from 1877 battlefields. Early accounts mention warriors wearing sandals of this type.

A3: Chief Maqoma, c.1835
Maqoma was the son of the early Xhosa hero Ngqika, and served as regent during the minority of Ngqika's heir, Sandile. Evicted from his lands by the British, and a bitter opponent of white expansion, he was a principal Xhosa leader in the Sixth and Eighth Wars, when his flair and daring greatly impressed his enemies. He is credited with having invented many of the Xhosa guerrilla tactics. He is shown here in the dress of a Xhosa chief—a leopardskin cloak and crane-feather headdress. Maqoma was a noted horseman.

A4: Cape Mounted Rifles renegade, c.1852
The Cape Mounted Rifles were one of the most important Colonial units used against the Xhosa in the Frontier Wars. In the Eighth War a number of troopers of Khoi descent—hitherto staunch allies of the Europeans—felt so aggrieved at their treatment by the Colonial authorities that they defected and joined the Xhosa. This man is wearing his CMR tunic, and carrying the double-barrelled carbine issued to the CMR for bush fighting. The remainder of his dress is the mix of European and African styles typical of the Khoi at this time.

A typical Boer leather bandolier, with flapped pouches containing Mauser clips. (National Army Museum)

B: The death of Chief Sandile, May 1878 (Ninth Frontier War)

B1: Ngqika (western Xhosa) warrior, 1877–78
The Ngqika were the Xhosa section most exposed to the Europeans, and by this time many had acquired European clothing and poor-quality guns. This man carries his shot in a traditional skin bag. He has been tending the chief's wounds; the Xhosa used grass to staunch the flow of blood. Other medical facilities consisted of herbal remedies, which had limited success on minor injuries, but were seldom effective against gunshot trauma.

B2: Chief Sandile
Sandile was chief of the Ngqika Xhosa from 1840. His left leg was withered by poliomyelitis; and he was well-known to whites as a brandy addict from his regular visits to frontier canteens. Nevertheless, when the 1877 war broke out he took to the field, and his spirited resistance made him a Xhosa hero. He was wounded in a skirmish with the Mfengu, who were fighting for the British in May 1878, and died several days later. His death marked the final collapse of Xhosa resistance. He is shown in the traditional dress of a Xhosa chief.

B3: Gcaleka (eastern Xhosa) warrior
The Gcaleka were heavily committed to the last Frontier War, but were severely defeated when they attacked the 1/24th Regiment in the open at the battle of Centane in February 1878. This is typical

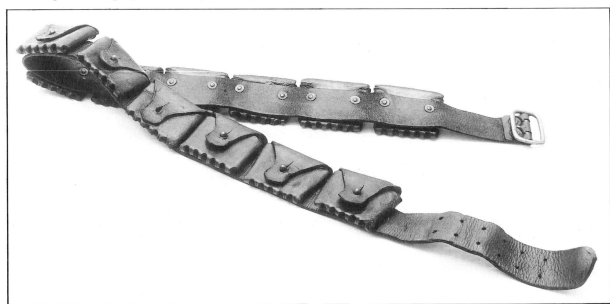

1896 pattern Mauser rifles—the standard Boer weapon of the Anglo-Boer War. (National Army Museum)

traditional Xhosa dress of the period: a trade blanket and black head-cloth. The black mark on the forehead and block of wood around the neck are magical charms intended to make the warrior brave and invincible.

C1: Basotho (southern Sotho) warrior

Most Basotho would have looked like this from the *mfecane* until the 1860s. His weapons are throwing spears and a club, with spares carried in a leather quiver. The small shield is typical of an ordinary warrior, as is the ostrich-plume headdress.

C2: Basotho chief, c.1850

The leopardskin cloak and striking metal gorget are indications of rank. The long plume of the shield was used as a standard in battle. The axe is of the pattern adopted from the Tlokwa. Traditional Basotho dress was worn during the wars of the 1850s and against the Orange Free State in the 1860s, but was dying out by the time of the Gun War.

C3: Basotho Warrior, Gun War, c.1880

By this time most Basotho were mounted on small 'Basotho ponies', and armed with some sort of firearm. The striped woollen blanket and high-crowned straw hat feature in many contemporary descriptions.

D1: Hlubi warrior, Langalibalele Rebellion, 1873

The majority of Hlubi warriors were probably dressed in this way during the skirmish at Bushman's Pass. The braided *iziyendane* hairstyle was once characteristic of the Hlubi, but by this time was just a young man's fashion. The rest of the dress and the weapons follow Zulu styles.

D2: Zulu warrior, Nokhenke ibutho (regiment), 1879

This man wears typical 'war dress'—an abbreviated form of regimental regalia. He retains a headband and cow tails around the legs; as well as a bag for percussion caps and a bandolier, he wears a wooden 'bravery bead' necklace indicating his prowess as a warrior, and a variety of magical charms around his neck. A high percentage of Zulu warriors carried firearms in the war of 1879. The Nokhenke *ibutho* formed part of the right horn at the battle of Isandlwana. They carried black shields, sometimes with white spots.

D3: Pedi warrior, Sekhukhune campaign, 1879

His breech-hide and cloak are typical Sotho costume, and he carries a mix of traditional and modern weapons—a knobkerry, axe and rifle. Because large numbers of Pedi had worked at Kimberley, they had acquired many firearms. Many probably also wore items of European clothing.

E: Ndebele warriors mustering in ceremonial regalia, c.1893

E1: Senior Ndebele warrior

Ndebele ('Matabele') *ndoda* (pl. *amadoda*) or senior warrior in typical dress. His costume retains considerable Zulu influence—note the otterskin headband with crane feathers. The kilt is of poor quality compared with the Zulu style, however. The headring, the symbol of a married man, is worn on the front of the crown. The *amadoda* spent most of their time living with their families, and were only

mustered in time of national need. This man's shield would probably have been white.

E2: Warrior of the Insuga regiment

Ndebele *ijaha* (pl. *amajaha*) or young warrior, of the Insuga *ibutho*. The Insuga were a Zansi (high caste) regiment, and were among King Lobengula's most aggressive; they took a prominent part in the battle of Shangani in 1893. This reconstruction shows the costume of a Zansi *ijaha* in all its finery: a waist-kilt and cape, circlet and pompon of black ostrich feathers.

E3: Warrior of the Imbizo regiment

The Imbizo were also a Zansi unit, the first formed by King Lobengula. They were great rivals of the younger Insuga. At the battle of Bembesi the Imbizo sustained a charge to within 100 yards of the Company's laager, and suffered appalling casualties as a result. Imbizo shields were white with black spots, and they seem to have worn a single white ostrich feather in their otherwise black headdress.

F1: Ndebele warrior, Holi caste

Although Holi *amajaha* theoretically wore the same costume as the higher classes, their lowly status was reflected in the poor quality of their costume.

Boer artillery at the Colenso battlefield, overlooking the Tugela River, December 1899. During the formal phase of the war, the Boers often defended natural features against British assault. (National Army Museum)

Ndebele commanders tended to regard Holi *amabutho* as poor fighting material, although there is no evidence that their battlefield performance was in fact disappointing.

F2: Ndebele warrior in 'war dress', 1893–6

Much of the ceremonial uniform was too fragile to wear into combat, but this ostrich-feather pompon does seem to have been retained. This man's loin covering of jackal-skin is typical of the Ndebele. The narrow binding on the shield is also characteristic of Ndebele styles, which evolved gradually from their Zulu origins.

F3: Rebel, 1896–7

Few Ndebele rebels would have worn regalia into battle in the 1896 Rebellion; many rebels, both Ndebele and Mashona, wore items of European clothing. Shona dress consisted of a hide breech-cloth. Both groups made extensive use of firearms.

G1: Boer Voortrekker, c.1842

The Trekkers fought hard campaigns against both African nations, such as the Ndebele and Zulu, and the British. This man's dress is typical of the period: a straw hat and short jacket, with powder-horn attached to the waist belt. His weapon is a civilian-pattern hunting gun. Behind him is *Ou Grietje*, a cannon improvised by the Trekkers by mounting a ship's gun on a carriage made from wagon parts. *Ou Grietje* is thought to have been used against the Zulus at the battle of Blood River in 1838, against Capt. Smith's fort at Port Natal in 1842, and was said to be in use as late as 1881.

G2: Commandant Andries Pretorius, c.1838

Pretorius was one of the Great Trek's most able military commanders, leading the Boers at Blood River, Port Natal and Boomplaats. This reconstruction is based on a portrait showing him at about the time of Blood River. His dark frock coat and top hat were typical of the clothing adopted by Boer leaders. Pretorius also carried a sword as a symbol of his authority.

G3: Boer, 1881

He carries a Westley-Richards falling-block carbine, with his cartridges in a looped bandolier. Compare the style of clothes with F1. Men such as this were able to rout Colley's professional soldiers at Majuba.

H1: Boer Commandant, 1899

In the early part of the Anglo-Boer War some commandants were still wearing the traditional top hat and tail coat. This habit died out, however, as the war became increasingly severe, and a younger generation of Boer leaders emerged.

H2: Boer, Transvaal Staats Artillerie

The Staats Artillerie was one of the very few Boer units to wear a uniform, although many members preferred some civilian items. This is the drab uniform worn in the field. The Staats Artillerie impressed the British with their professionalism as gunners; after they lost their ordnance towards the end of the formal stage of the war, they were

Boer generals of the Anglo-Boer War: (*l to r*) Lucas Meyer, Louis Botha and Erasmus. Although Meyer and Botha are wearing drab uniforms, most Boer commandants, like Erasmus, preferred civilian dress. (National Army Museum)

reorganised as a mounted unit, and fought as commandos.

H3: Boer commando, 1899–1902

Most Boers wore their civilian clothes throughout the war—this man's appearance is typical. He carries a Mauser semi-automatic pistol with a wooden holster-stock, which was highly regarded by those Boers who could afford such a luxury. Note the bandolier designed to carry cartridge clips in flapped pouches.

H4: 'Bitter-Ender', 1902

By the end of the guerrilla war many Boers were suffering severe hardship from the war of attrition. It was common for worn-out clothing to be replaced by items taken from dead or captured British soldiers, despite the fact that the British shot many who did so as spies. This man is wearing a mix of captured British and civilian clothes, and his appearance reflects the rigours of prolonged exposure to the extremes of the South African elements.

Notes sur les planches en couleur

A1 Ce guerrier Xhosa porta la tenue traditionnelle; notez sa lance avec pointe métallique aiguisée au lieu d'une lame. **A2** La coiffure en plumes d'aile grises que porte cet homme marque probablement sa jeunesse et son inexpérience. **A3** Le Chef Maqoma est vêtu comme il sied à son rang d'un manteau en peau de léopard et d'une coiffure en plumes de grue. **A4** Cet homme porte l'uniforme des Cape Mounted Rifles, bien qu'avec d'autres soldats de lignée Khoi révoltés par leur condition, il se batte pour les Xhosa.

B1 Ce guerrier Ngqika, soignant les blessures de son chef, a acquis des vêtements européens, bien qu'il porte son fusil dans un sac en peau traditionnel. **B2** Sandile, qui porte la tenue d'un chef Xhosa, prit la tête de son peuple dans la guerre de 1877 malgré ses souffrances physiques. **B3** La couverture traditionnelle et le turban noir faisait partie de la tenue Xhosa courante à cette époque. La marque sur le front et l'amulette en bois au cou sont des fétiches magiques.

C1 Cet homme porte un petit bouclier de guerrier et une coiffure en plumes d'autruche, comme armes des lances et un bâton. **C2** La longue plume du bouclier du chef était caractéristique en bataille. **C3** Il existe de nombreuses descriptions datant de cette époque de Basotho à cheval portant de hauts chapeaux de paille et des couvertures rayées.

D1 La tenue des guerriers Hlubi et leurs armes étaient semblables aux styles Zoulous; la coiffure à nattes était à la mode pour les jeunes gens. **D2** Cet homme porte la tenue de guerre caractéristique des Zoulous et un bouclier du régiment Nokhenke—noir, à points blancs parfois. **D3** Ce guerrier Pedi porte un mélange d'armes traditionnelles et modernes; il porte le costume Sotho caractéristique.

E1 Vieux guerrier Ndebele, il porte un kilt de pauvre qualité et un anneau de coiffure sur le devant de la tête—notez la forte influence Zoulou. **E2** Les Insuga étaient un régiment de caste élevée; ce guerrier est présenté dans son plus beau costume. **E3** Les Imbizo se distinguaient par leurs boucliers blancs et la plume unique blanche dans leurs coiffures noires.

F1 Le statut inférieur de cette unité se voit d'après la pauvre qualité du costume de ce guerrier Ndebele. **F2** La majeure partie de ce costume de cérémonie était trop fragile pour être portée en bataille—seule la plume d'autruche était conservée. **F3** De nombreux rebelles portaient des vêtements européens en 1896 et avaient des armes à feu.

G1 Ce Trekker porte le chapeau de paille et la veste courte caractéristiques. Vous pouvez voir derrière lui le célèbre canon 'Ou Grietje', employé pour la première fois à Blood River en 1838 et toujours en service en 1881. **G2** D'après un portrait d'époque, Pretorius porte à son rang d'une épée, symbole de son autorité. **G3** Ce Boer porte une carabine Westley-Richards.

H1 Au début de la guerre des Boers, les commandants portaient encore des chapeaux hauts et des habits queue-de-pie. **H2** L'artillerie Staats était l'une de quelques unités Boers à porter un uniforme. La plupart des Boers portaient des vêtements civils comme **H3**. Notex son Mauser, pistolet semi-automatique, avec étui en bois et bandoulière conçue pour transporter des chargeurs dans des poches à rabat.

Farbtafeln

A1 Dieser Xhosa-Krieger trägt die traditionelle Bekleidung; interessant ist der Speer mit der spitzen Metallzacke anstelle einer Schneide. **A2** Die graue Kopfbedeckung mit Flügelfedern bedeutet wahrscheinlich, dass der Träger ein junger, unerfahrener Mann ist. **A3** Maqoma, der Stammesälteste, ist standesgemäss mit einem Leopardenumhang und einer Kopfbedeckung aus Kranichfedern gekleidet. **A4** Dieser Mann trägt die Uniform der Cape Mounted Rifles. Auch andere Soldaten, die von den Khoi abstammten, kämpften für die Xhosa, da sie sich durch ihre Kolonialherren schlecht behandelt fühlten.

B1 Dieser Ngqika Krieger—in europäischer Kleidung—versorgt die Wunde des Stammesältesten. Im üblichen Fellbeutel werden die Schrottkugeln aufbewahrt. **B2** Sandile, im Gewand des Stammesältesten der Xhosa, führte seinen Stamm 1877 im Krieg gegen die Briten, trotz schwerer Verletzungen. **B3** Eine Handelsdecke und die Kopfbedeckung aus schwarzem Stoff war bei den Xhosa damals üblich. Das Zeichen auf der Stirn und das hölzerne Amulett am Hals sind vermeintlich schützende oder glücksbringende Talismane.

C1 Dieser Mann verfügt über ein kleines Kriegerschild und trägt eine Kopfbeckung aus Straussenfedern. Seine Bewaffnung setzt sich aus einem Speer und einer Keule zusammen. **C2** Die lange Feder am Schild des Stammesältesten wurde im Kampf immer verwendet. **C3** Es existieren unzählige zeitgenössische Beschreibungen über berittene Basotho mit hochgezogenen Strohhütten und gestreiften Decken.

D1 Das Gewand der Hlubi Krieger und ihre Waffen war dem der Zulu ähnlich; junge Männer hatten geflochtenes Haar. **D2** Dieser Mann ist in der typischen Zulu-Kriegsbekleidung zu sehen und hat ein Schild des Nikhenke Regiments, welches in schwarz und manchmal mit weissen Punkten gehalten wurde. **D3** Ein Pedi Krieger mit einer Mischung aus traditionellen und modernen Waffen; gekleidet ist er im typischen Sotho-Gewand.

E1 Ein ältere Ndebele Krieger, der einen minderwertigen Kilt und ein Kopfband trägt; bemerkenswert ist der starke Zulu-Einfluss. **E2** Die Insuga waren das Regiment einer hochstehenden Kaste; dieser Krieger ist in seinem besten Gewand abgebildet. **E3** Die Imbizo unterschieden sich durch ihre weissen Schilder mit schwarzen Punkten sowie einer einzigen weissen Feder in ihrer schwarzen Kopfbedeckung.

F1 Die niedere Stellung dieser Einheit wird durch die minderwertige Qualität des Gewandes dieses Ndebele Kriegers deutlich. **F2** Der Grossteil des Zeremoniekostüms war zu empfindlich, um es im Kampf zu tragen; nur die Straussenfeder wurde beibehalten. **F3** Viele Rebellen trugen europäische Kleidung im Jahr 1896 und Feuerwaffen.

G1 Dieser Trakker trägt den typischen Strohhut und die kurze Jacke. Hinter ihm ist die berühmte 'Ou Grietje' Kanone zu sehen, die erstmals am Blood River im Jahre 1838 zum Einsatz gelangte und auch noch bis 1881 benutzt wurde. **G2** Beruhend auf einem zeitgenössischen Portrait, trägt Pretorious die vom Burenführer übernommene Bekleidung und hat ein Schwert, das seine Autorität symbolisiert. **G3** Dieser Bure ist mit einem Westley-Richards Karabiner ausgerüstet.

H1 Zu Beginn des Burenkrieges trugen die Kommandanten Zylinderhüte und einen Frack. **H2** Nur die Staats Artillerie war eine der wenigen Bureneinheiten, die Uniformen trugen. Die meisten Buren waren normal gekleidet. **H3** Auffallend ist diese halb-automatische Pistole mit hölzernem Halfter und dem Patronengurt, um die Ladestreifen in eine Patronentasche mit Klappe zu tun.